Ask And You Shall
Receive

Daily Asking Journal

"**Ask**, and it will be given to you; **seek** and you will find; **knock** and the door will be opened to you. For everyone who asks receives; the one who seeks finds; and to the one who knocks, the door will be opened."

—Matthew 7:7-8 (NIV)

This Daily Asking Journal belongs to and is prayed over

By: _____   Date: _____

Rediscover Truth

Ask And You Shall Receive
Daily Asking Journal
Receive Joy

Receive Joy Publishing
Naples, Florida, U.S.A.

ISBN: 978-0-9988484-0-2

Receive Joy
www.receivejoy.com
ask@receivejoy.com

YOUR GUIDE FOR USING
THE DAILY ASKING JOURNAL

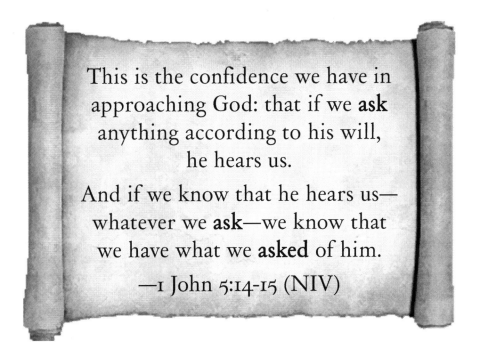

This is the confidence we have in approaching God: that if we **ask** anything according to his will, he hears us.

And if we know that he hears us— whatever we **ask**—we know that we have what we **asked** of him.

—1 John 5:14-15 (NIV)

Now that you have read the book *Ask And You Shall Receive* by Receive Joy let us put the Nine Step Method into daily action. To make your daily asking light and easy, Receive Joy created this *Daily Asking Journal*. Your journal will help you connect with the Power of the Universe, enabling you to focus on and physically create your asking intentions.

The intention of the *Ask And You Shall Receive Daily Asking Journal* is to have all positive thoughts and words collected, organized, and recorded in one place. This helps you to raise your awareness and have an organized platform to consciously create and record your positive, happy, light, and easy life.

Take time to journal each day, preferably at the close of the day or first thing in the morning. Script your life and be God's new wineskin.

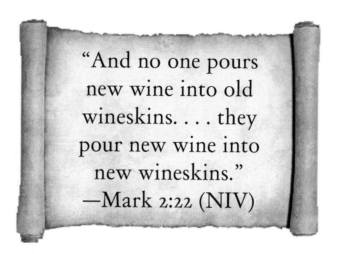

"And no one pours new wine into old wineskins. . . . they pour new wine into new wineskins."
—Mark 2:22 (NIV)

HOW TO JOURNAL DAILY

1. Fill in today's date.

2. Read the daily inspiration and receive joy. Be blessed with fresh inspiration for your day.

3. Thank God and list whatever you are grateful for in the box labeled "I am grateful for". Please include people, events, and circumstances. What aspects in your life are you thankful for? What went well today? Remember to include personal features and emotions. Allow this list to grow and grow every day. Read through your accumulated gratitude and feel your spirit lifted as often as desired.

4. Take a Five Minute Couch Time during your day to ponder a specific question you have and listen to the inspired answers you receive, or take time now and reflect on your day. Ask yourself: What may I do differently to allow more peace to flow into my life? What additional consciousness and acceptance shall I welcome in for me to be God's new wineskin? Write your answer on the lines provided.

5. List one action that you will take in the next 24 hours to celebrate this day. Select something you find joyful and fun. Play your Game of Fun, roll the dice, and choose the rewarding activity you land on.

6. Now, let us focus on the **asking**. Fill in all the lines in the box labeled "I ask with intention for". **Ask** for whatever you desire to consciously create and receive. Please remember to use only positive words. Knock three times: think it, speak it, and write it down as if it is already here. Ideally, state new intentions each day. Remember, God already has received yesterday's intentions. State your intentions that are still in the making over again if it helps to strengthen your belief and builds your confidence. Be graciously aware that you can change your goals in any way at any time in the future. Also remember to dream bigger. To ask in more detail, there are pages provided in the back of the book to define all the parameters you wish to include for your creation process.

7. To fuel your emotion and accelerate the delivery of your creation, **ask** yourself why you desire what you **asked** for with intention. Go deep inside yourself and listen to your gut feeling until the true why is revealed to you. Make a note of your inspired thoughts in the box "Why?"

8. The next box to focus on is "My goals achieved and miracles created". This box is available to help you think back over your day and count your blessings. Be aware of all thoughts and words you are sending out and what is being attracted back to you and now is manifesting in your life. This constant awareness helps you to deepen your belief and motivates your daily conscious asking. Keep score of your creation power by filling out this box.

9. Fill out your daily "sticky note" by listing five things you wish to accomplish and focus on throughout the day. You may wish to use a pack of sticky notes and stick the note with today's five ideas directly on the cover of your journal to bring along to your daily Breakfast with God.

10. Read the sentence underneath the boxes as a constant reminder to praise God. Give Him all the glory. Remember to stay in a state of joy and happiness always. Be fully aware of your breath as it is God's gift to you.

11. Check the box "☑ I read my Bible" after you have read your daily devotion or verse of the day.

12. Check the box "☑ I am connected to God" after you aligned your head with your heart and have listened to your gut feeling. Be joyously aware that we are always in His presence. Empowering ways to stay connected to the Power of the Universe are described in Receive Joy's book *Connect To The Light* (ISBN 9780998848419).

13. Check the box "☑ I meditated for 15 minutes" after you have completed your meditation.

14. Read through your entire page again to edit your words. Make sure that you stated everything in **positive words** and in the **present tense**. When you feel joyfully assured that this is exactly what you wish to create check the box "☑ I edited my words three times".

15. Take a moment to rejoice and pray with love and gratitude. Pray over everything you wrote on today's page and whatever else is on your heart.

"Seek ye **first** the Kingdom
of Heaven (God) and
his righteousness; and
all these things shall be
added unto you."
—Matthew 6:33 (KJV)

16. Have someone else second the motion. Call or meet your prayer partner for encouragement. Check the box "second the motion" or have someone initial the box. Remember, the combined energies of two or more are greater than a single energy.

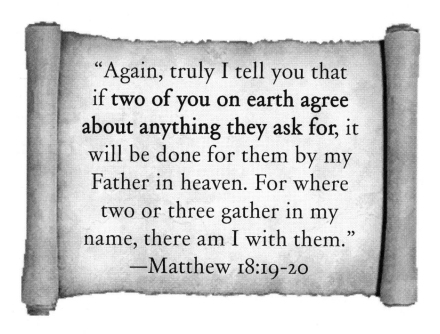

"Again, truly I tell you that if **two of you on earth agree about anything they ask for,** it will be done for them by my Father in heaven. For where two or three gather in my name, there am I with them."
—Matthew 18:19-20

To have a better visual of the process, a sample page is provided.

Ideally, this quarterly journal is filled with each new season's asking intentions. Build your asking muscle by using it every day. Take the journal with you and constantly continue your asking.

Declare everything in writing before you take action.

Ask, Ask, Ask!

In the last quarter of this *Daily Asking Journal* you will find pages to fill in to help you clarify and define your intentional asking. What do you expect to receive? How can you make each goal a Ten Star Experience? Be excited about receiving your manifestations.

Each Declaration Page is to be filled out in four parts:

1. Start by writing your intention in the lines provided that start with "I declare that". Continue with "I am," "I allow," or "I have" and finish the sentence as if you have already received your asking.

2. Define your parameters to ask and create with detail. List the details of your asking. What components do you desire to be included? What ingredients are an absolute requirement to form your custom goal? Add as many parameters as you can think of. Eight details are perfect, more are preferred.

3. Take a moment to enter inside yourself to discover the motivation for your desire. Then articulate in writing why you desire this intention or goal. Why is this desire important to you? Does it make you feel good? Will it be helpful to you? What does having this mean to you? Fill out the line provided under "Why?"

4. Pray over your page and give gratitude to God, Jesus, and the Holy Spirit. Fill out the lines underneath to share love, gratitude, and thanks with everyone you wish to include.

5. Have the page seconded and initialed by your prayer partner or a friend who encourages you.

A sample page is provided up front.

Copy one of the pages if you have more desires than pages provided. Ideally, every single important conscious creation deserves a whole page defining its parameters. Being detailed in your desires and answering why it is important to you increases the focus on the intention. Visualizing your actualized goal and being joyfully excited enables you to send out an elevated intentional frequency to match your desire. Everything in your life shall be a miraculous Ten Star Experience. Create your desired experience on paper first. These pages build the stage for your life. Script your life and write your own story!

Tape notes, photos, and pictures in your journal. Included at the end of the journal are blank "Notes" pages giving you ample space to be creative in your asking as you collect your ideas and inspirations.

The process of writing down your goals and intentions allows creativity to become a reality in its physical form. Let us write everything down! Let us journal daily! Let us consciously **ask** and **receive** our joy!

To God be the glory!

With Love and Gratitude,

Receive Joy

Rediscover Truth

MY DIVINE MISSION

Write down your divine mission and life's purpose to be constantly aware of it. In case you are still searching for your life's mission, take the time right now to define yourself. Refer to pages 149 to 154 of the book *Ask And You Shall Receive* by Receive Joy to help you find your purpose. We came into this awesome world filled with love and now we are here with the opportunity to experience this love and and light for ourselves and to share it with others.

My divine mission is _____

_____

_____

_____

_____

_____

_____

_____

_____

_____

MY MONTHLY GOALS

My goals for the month of _____

_____
_____
_____
_____
_____
_____
_____
_____
_____
_____
_____
_____
_____
_____
_____
_____
_____
_____
_____
_____
_____
_____

I vividly see myself with my goals obtained and miracles created!

_____   _____
        Signature   Date

MY MONTHLY GOALS

My goals for the month of _____

_____
_____
_____
_____
_____
_____
_____
_____
_____
_____
_____
_____
_____
_____
_____
_____
_____
_____
_____
_____
_____

I vividly see myself with my goals obtained and miracles created!

_____   _____
             Signature   Date

MY MONTHLY GOALS

My goals for the month of _____

_____

_____

_____

_____

_____

_____

_____

_____

_____

_____

_____

_____

_____

_____

_____

_____

_____

_____

_____

_____

I vividly see myself with my goals obtained and miracles created!

_____   _____

Signature   Date

Date: ___today___

I choose to feel excellent about myself. I make this choice every morning.

I am grateful for:
my amazing loving family
all the wonderful people in my life
my loving pets
my light and easy life
miracles in every moment
my creator and savior

What may I do differently to allow more happiness and peace in my life?
I smile, laugh, and show
more love to everyone I meet
during the day

I have fun and celebrate this day by:
taking a bath with candlelight

I ask with intention for:
relaxing beach vacation with my family
perfect health and my neck moving freely
continual financial abundance
a comfortable cute swim suit
I am accepted at the university of my choice,
   all paid in full
all A's this semester   and more!

Why?
I love myself as God
   loves me
I deserve it
it makes me happy
I enjoy swimming
the more I receive the
   more I can give

My gains and miracles created:
I have the perfect gift for my sister
I bought the perfect car for me
I won the raffle at the club
my loan is paid in full
I swam with manatees

1 call my best friend
2 gym — 1 hour of exercise
3 family dinner
4 purchase a new printer
5 take my car in for service

To God be the glory! I rejoice always! Thank you for my breath of life.

☑ I read my Bible.

☑ I am connected to God.

☑ I meditated for 15 min.

☑ I edited my words three times.

☑ I prayed.

☺

second the motion

RJ

Date: 10-28-19

I now joyfully accept and appreciate the abundant life
the Universe offers me.

I am grateful for:
learning to Play tennis
With Kaia

What may I do differently to allow more
happiness and peace in my life?
Calm Cool - Collective

I have fun and celebrate this day by:
Playing with Kaid

I ask with intention for:
a New house
a New Car
a New Job
New New New

_____ and more!

Why?
Out wth the
Old IN with
New
We deserve.

My gains and miracles created:
Switch with come early

1 _____
2 _____
3 _____
4 _____
5 _____

To God be the glory! I rejoice always! Thank you for my breath of life.

❑ I read my Bible.

❑ I am connected to God.

❑ I meditated for 15 min.

❑ I edited my words three times.

❑ I prayed.

☺

second the motion

Date: _____

I flow with all that life offers me in every moment.

I am grateful for:
_____
_____
_____
_____
_____

What may I do differently to allow more happiness and peace in my life?
_____
_____
_____

I have fun and celebrate this day by:
_____

I ask with intention for:
_____
_____
_____
_____
_____
_____ and more!

Why?
_____
_____
_____
_____
_____

My gains and miracles created:
_____
_____
_____
_____

1 _____
2 _____
3 _____
4 _____
5 _____

To God be the glory! I rejoice always! Thank you for my breath of life.

❑ I read my Bible.

❑ I am connected to God.

❑ I meditated for 15 min.

❑ I edited my words three times.

❑ I prayed.

☺

second the motion

Date: _____

I am the co-creator of my own life and
I act with grace and mercy in all I do.

I am grateful for:	What may I do differently to allow more happiness and peace in my life?
_____	_____
_____	_____
_____	_____
_____	**I have fun and celebrate this day by:**
_____	_____

I ask with intention for:	Why?
_____	_____
_____	_____
_____	_____
_____	_____
_____	_____
_____ and more!	_____

My gains and miracles created:	
_____	1 _____
_____	2 _____
_____	3 _____
_____	4 _____
_____	5 _____

To God be the glory! I rejoice always! Thank you for my breath of life.

❏ I read my Bible.

❏ I am connected to God.

❏ I meditated for 15 min.

❏ I edited my words three times.

❏ I prayed.

☺

second the motion ☐

Date: _____

I am a true blessing.

I am grateful for:	What may I do differently to allow more happiness and peace in my life?
_____ _____ _____ _____ _____	_____ _____ _____
	I have fun and celebrate this day by: _____

I ask with intention for:	Why?
_____ _____ _____ _____ _____ _____ and more!	_____ _____ _____ _____ _____ _____

My gains and miracles created:	
_____ _____ _____ _____	1 _____ 2 _____ 3 _____ 4 _____ 5 _____

To God be the glory! I rejoice always! Thank you for my breath of life.

❑ I read my Bible.

❑ I am connected to God.

❑ I meditated for 15 min.

❑ I edited my words three times.

❑ I prayed.

☺

second the motion ⬚

Date: _____

My day is all planned out the night before. I know my next step.

I am grateful for:	What may I do differently to allow more happiness and peace in my life?
_____	_____
_____	_____
_____	_____
_____	I have fun and celebrate this day by:
_____	_____

I ask with intention for:	Why?
_____	_____
_____	_____
_____	_____
_____	_____
_____	_____
_____ and more!	_____

My gains and miracles created:	
_____	1 _____
_____	2 _____
_____	3 _____
_____	4 _____
_____	5 _____

To God be the glory! I rejoice always! Thank you for my breath of life.

❑ I read my Bible.

❑ I am connected to God.

❑ I meditated for 15 min.

❑ I edited my words three times.

❑ I prayed.

☺

second the motion

Date: _____

I choose to feel excellent about myself. I make this choice every morning.

I am grateful for:	What may I do differently to allow more happiness and peace in my life?
_____	_____
_____	_____
_____	_____
_____	**I have fun and celebrate this day by:**
_____	_____

I ask with intention for:	Why?
_____	_____
_____	_____
_____	_____
_____	_____
_____	_____
_____ and more!	_____

My gains and miracles created:	
_____	1 _____
_____	2 _____
_____	3 _____
_____	4 _____
_____	5 _____

To God be the glory! I rejoice always! Thank you for my breath of life.

- ❏ I read my Bible.
- ❏ I am connected to God.
- ❏ I meditated for 15 min.
- ❏ I edited my words three times.
- ❏ I prayed.

☺

second the motion ☐

Date: _____

I am the child of God.

I am grateful for:	What may I do differently to allow more happiness and peace in my life?
_____	_____
_____	_____
_____	_____
_____	**I have fun and celebrate this day by:**
_____	_____

I ask with intention for:	Why?
_____	_____
_____	_____
_____	_____
_____	_____
_____	_____
_____ and more!	_____

My gains and miracles created:	
_____	1 _____
_____	2 _____
_____	3 _____
_____	4 _____
_____	5 _____

To God be the glory! I rejoice always! Thank you for my breath of life.

❑ I read my Bible.

❑ I am connected to God.

❑ I meditated for 15 min.

❑ I edited my words three times.

❑ I prayed.

☺

second the motion ⬜

Date: _____

I have all the resources I desire. I am resourceful.

I am grateful for:
_____
_____
_____
_____
_____
_____

What may I do differently to allow more happiness and peace in my life?
_____
_____
_____

I have fun and celebrate this day by:
_____

I ask with intention for:
_____
_____
_____
_____
_____
_____ and more!

Why?
_____
_____
_____
_____
_____
_____

My gains and miracles created:
_____
_____
_____
_____

1 _____
2 _____
3 _____
4 _____
5 _____

To God be the glory! I rejoice always! Thank you for my breath of life.

❑ I read my Bible.

❑ I am connected to God.

❑ I meditated for 15 min.

❑ I edited my words three times.

❑ I prayed.

☺

second the motion ☐

Date: _____

I have faith, I believe. My heart is at peace.

I am grateful for:	What may I do differently to allow more happiness and peace in my life?
_____	_____
_____	_____
_____	_____
_____	**I have fun and celebrate this day by:**
_____	_____

I ask with intention for:	Why?
_____	_____
_____	_____
_____	_____
_____	_____
_____	_____
_____ and more!	_____

My gains and miracles created:	
_____	1 _____
_____	2 _____
_____	3 _____
_____	4 _____
_____	5 _____

To God be the glory! I rejoice always! Thank you for my breath of life.

❑   I read my Bible.

❑   I am connected to God.

❑   I meditated for 15 min.

❑   I edited my words three times.

❑   I prayed.

☺

second the motion

Date: _____

My life continues to be better and better. I grow into the greater good.

I am grateful for:	What may I do differently to allow more happiness and peace in my life?
_____	_____
_____	_____
_____	_____
_____	**I have fun and celebrate this day by:**
_____	_____

I ask with intention for:	Why?
_____	_____
_____	_____
_____	_____
_____	_____
_____	_____
_____ and more!	_____

My gains and miracles created:	
_____	1 _____
_____	2 _____
_____	3 _____
_____	4 _____
_____	5 _____

To God be the glory! I rejoice always! Thank you for my breath of life.

❑ I read my Bible.

❑ I am connected to God.

❑ I meditated for 15 min.

❑ I edited my words three times.

❑ I prayed.

☺

second the motion

Date: _____

I allow all that is good in and it flows joyfully.

I am grateful for:
_____
_____
_____
_____
_____

What may I do differently to allow more happiness and peace in my life?
_____
_____
_____

I have fun and celebrate this day by:
_____

I ask with intention for:
_____
_____
_____
_____
_____
_____ and more!

Why?
_____
_____
_____
_____
_____
_____

My gains and miracles created:
_____
_____
_____
_____
_____

1 _____
2 _____
3 _____
4 _____
5 _____

To God be the glory! I rejoice always! Thank you for my breath of life.

❑ I read my Bible.

❑ I am connected to God.

❑ I meditated for 15 min.

❑ I edited my words three times.

❑ I prayed.

☺

second the motion

Date: _____

I only speak positive and loving words.
I know my words create everything.

I am grateful for:
_____
_____
_____
_____
_____

What may I do differently to allow more happiness and peace in my life?
_____
_____
_____

I have fun and celebrate this day by:
_____

I ask with intention for:
_____
_____
_____
_____
_____
_____ and more!

Why?
_____
_____
_____
_____
_____

My gains and miracles created:
_____
_____
_____
_____
_____

1 _____
2 _____
3 _____
4 _____
5 _____

To God be the glory! I rejoice always! Thank you for my breath of life.

❑ I read my Bible.

❑ I am connected to God.

❑ I meditated for 15 min.

❑ I edited my words three times.

❑ I prayed.

☺

second the motion ☐

Date: _____

I choose to see the highest good in everyone.

I am grateful for:	What may I do differently to allow more happiness and peace in my life?
_____	_____
_____	_____
_____	_____
_____	**I have fun and celebrate this day by:**
_____	_____

I ask with intention for:	Why?
_____	_____
_____	_____
_____	_____
_____	_____
_____	_____
_____ and more!	_____

My gains and miracles created:	
_____	1 _____
_____	2 _____
_____	3 _____
_____	4 _____
_____	5 _____

To God be the glory! I rejoice always! Thank you for my breath of life.

❑ I read my Bible.

❑ I am connected to God.

❑ I meditated for 15 min.

❑ I edited my words three times.

❑ I prayed.

☺

second the motion ▢

Date: _____

I am grateful for this perfect day.

I am grateful for:
_____
_____
_____
_____
_____
_____

What may I do differently to allow more happiness and peace in my life?
_____
_____
_____

I have fun and celebrate this day by:
_____

I ask with intention for:
_____
_____
_____
_____
_____
_____ and more!

Why?
_____
_____
_____
_____
_____
_____

My gains and miracles created:
_____
_____
_____
_____
_____

1 _____
2 _____
3 _____
4 _____
5 _____

To God be the glory! I rejoice always! Thank you for my breath of life.

❑ I read my Bible.
❑ I am connected to God.
❑ I meditated for 15 min.
❑ I edited my words three times.
❑ I prayed.

☺

second the motion

Date: _____

I am successful. I surround myself with amazing, successful people.

I am grateful for:	What may I do differently to allow more happiness and peace in my life?
_____	_____
_____	_____
_____	_____
_____	**I have fun and celebrate this day by:**
_____	_____

I ask with intention for:	Why?
_____	_____
_____	_____
_____	_____
_____	_____
_____	_____
_____ and more!	_____

My gains and miracles created:	
_____	1 _____
_____	2 _____
_____	3 _____
_____	4 _____
_____	5 _____

To God be the glory! I rejoice always! Thank you for my breath of life.

❑ I read my Bible.

❑ I am connected to God.

❑ I meditated for 15 min.

❑ I edited my words three times.

❑ I prayed.

☺

second the motion

Date: _____

I smile constantly.

I am grateful for:
_____
_____
_____
_____
_____
_____

What may I do differently to allow more happiness and peace in my life?
_____
_____
_____

I have fun and celebrate this day by:
_____

I ask with intention for:
_____
_____
_____
_____
_____
_____ and more!

Why?
_____
_____
_____
_____
_____
_____

My gains and miracles created:
_____
_____
_____
_____

1 _____
2 _____
3 _____
4 _____
5 _____

To God be the glory! I rejoice always! Thank you for my breath of life.

❑ I read my Bible.
❑ I am connected to God.
❑ I meditated for 15 min.
❑ I edited my words three times.
❑ I prayed.

☺

second the motion

Date: _____

I understand that my life's path is up to me.

I am grateful for:	What may I do differently to allow more happiness and peace in my life?
_____	_____
_____	_____
_____	_____
_____	**I have fun and celebrate this day by:**
_____	_____

I ask with intention for:	Why?
_____	_____
_____	_____
_____	_____
_____	_____
_____	_____
_____ and more!	_____

My gains and miracles created:	
_____	1 _____
_____	2 _____
_____	3 _____
_____	4 _____
_____	5 _____

To God be the glory! I rejoice always! Thank you for my breath of life.

❑ I read my Bible.

❑ I am connected to God.

❑ I meditated for 15 min.

❑ I edited my words three times.

❑ I prayed.

☺

second the motion [ ]

Date: _____

*I focus on positive thoughts and blessed words, because the thoughts
I think attract and the words I speak create.*

I am grateful for:	What may I do differently to allow more happiness and peace in my life?
_____	_____
_____	_____
_____	_____
_____	I have fun and celebrate this day by:
_____	_____

I ask with intention for:	Why?
_____	_____
_____	_____
_____	_____
_____	_____
_____	_____
_____ and more!	_____

My gains and miracles created:	
_____	1 _____
_____	2 _____
_____	3 _____
_____	4 _____
_____	5 _____

To God be the glory! I rejoice always! Thank you for my breath of life.

❑ I read my Bible.

❑ I am connected to God.

❑ I meditated for 15 min.

❑ I edited my words three times.

❑ I prayed.

☺

second the motion ▢

Date: _____

My life is light and easy.

I am grateful for:	What may I do differently to allow more happiness and peace in my life?
_____	_____
_____	_____
_____	_____
_____	**I have fun and celebrate this day by:**
_____	_____

I ask with intention for:	Why?
_____	_____
_____	_____
_____	_____
_____	_____
_____	_____
_____ and more!	_____

My gains and miracles created:	
_____	1 _____
_____	2 _____
_____	3 _____
_____	4 _____
_____	5 _____

To God be the glory! I rejoice always! Thank you for my breath of life.

❑ I read my Bible.

❑ I am connected to God.

❑ I meditated for 15 min.

❑ I edited my words three times.

❑ I prayed.

☺

second the motion ☐

Date: _____

I love myself. I love my life. I allow my love to flow freely.

I am grateful for:	What may I do differently to allow more happiness and peace in my life?
_____	_____
_____	_____
_____	_____
_____	**I have fun and celebrate this day by:**
_____	_____

I ask with intention for:	Why?
_____	_____
_____	_____
_____	_____
_____	_____
_____	_____
_____ and more!	_____

My gains and miracles created:	
_____	1 _____
_____	2 _____
_____	3 _____
_____	4 _____
_____	5 _____

To God be the glory! I rejoice always! Thank you for my breath of life.

❑ I read my Bible.

❑ I am connected to God.

❑ I meditated for 15 min.

❑ I edited my words three times.

❑ I prayed.

☺

second the motion ⬜

Date: _____

I am a rejoicing soul.

I am grateful for:	What may I do differently to allow more happiness and peace in my life?
_____	_____
_____	_____
_____	_____
_____	**I have fun and celebrate this day by:**
_____	_____

I ask with intention for:	Why?
_____	_____
_____	_____
_____	_____
_____	_____
_____	_____
_____ and more!	_____

My gains and miracles created:	
_____	1 _____
_____	2 _____
_____	3 _____
_____	4 _____
_____	5 _____

To God be the glory! I rejoice always! Thank you for my breath of life.

❑ I read my Bible.

❑ I am connected to God.

❑ I meditated for 15 min.

❑ I edited my words three times.

❑ I prayed.

☺

second the motion ☐

Date: _____

By faith I declare all my actions before I take them.
I declare the exact outcome for all my actions.

I am grateful for:	What may I do differently to allow more happiness and peace in my life?
_____	_____
_____	_____
_____	_____
_____	**I have fun and celebrate this day by:**
_____	_____

I ask with intention for:	Why?
_____	_____
_____	_____
_____	_____
_____	_____
_____	_____
_____ and more!	_____

My gains and miracles created:	
_____	1 _____
_____	2 _____
_____	3 _____
_____	4 _____
_____	5 _____

To God be the glory! I rejoice always! Thank you for my breath of life.

❑ I read my Bible.

❑ I am connected to God.

❑ I meditated for 15 min.

❑ I edited my words three times.

❑ I prayed.

☺

second the motion ⬜

Date: _____

I am living a life of abundance, happiness, and wealth.

I am grateful for:	What may I do differently to allow more happiness and peace in my life?
_____	_____
_____	_____
_____	_____
_____	**I have fun and celebrate this day by:**
_____	_____

I ask with intention for:	Why?
_____	_____
_____	_____
_____	_____
_____	_____
_____	_____
_____ and more!	_____

My gains and miracles created:	
_____	1 _____
_____	2 _____
_____	3 _____
_____	4 _____
_____	5 _____

To God be the glory! I rejoice always! Thank you for my breath of life.

❑ I read my Bible.

❑ I am connected to God.

❑ I meditated for 15 min.

❑ I edited my words three times.

❑ I prayed.

☺

second the motion ☐

Date: _____

My body is perfect. I am vibrant and healthy. I feel energized.

I am grateful for:
_____
_____
_____
_____
_____
_____

What may I do differently to allow more happiness and peace in my life?
_____
_____
_____

I have fun and celebrate this day by:
_____

I ask with intention for:
_____
_____
_____
_____
_____
_____ and more!

Why?
_____
_____
_____
_____
_____
_____

My gains and miracles created:
_____
_____
_____
_____
_____

1 _____
2 _____
3 _____
4 _____
5 _____

To God be the glory! I rejoice always! Thank you for my breath of life.

❑ I read my Bible.
❑ I am connected to God.
❑ I meditated for 15 min.
❑ I edited my words three times.
❑ I prayed.

☺

second the motion

Date: _____

I expect only great things in my life.

I am grateful for:	What may I do differently to allow more happiness and peace in my life?
_____	_____
_____	_____
_____	_____
_____	**I have fun and celebrate this day by:**
_____	_____

I ask with intention for:	Why?
_____	_____
_____	_____
_____	_____
_____	_____
_____	_____
_____ and more!	_____

My gains and miracles created:	
_____	1 _____
_____	2 _____
_____	3 _____
_____	4 _____
_____	5 _____

To God be the glory! I rejoice always! Thank you for my breath of life.

❑ I read my Bible.

❑ I am connected to God.

❑ I meditated for 15 min.

❑ I edited my words three times.

❑ I prayed.

☺

second the motion ☐

Date: _____

I am fulfilled. I know that my desires are taken care of.

I am grateful for:	What may I do differently to allow more happiness and peace in my life?
_____	_____
_____	_____
_____	_____
_____	**I have fun and celebrate this day by:**
_____	_____

I ask with intention for:	Why?
_____	_____
_____	_____
_____	_____
_____	_____
_____	_____
_____ and more!	_____

My gains and miracles created:	
_____	1 _____
_____	2 _____
_____	3 _____
_____	4 _____
_____	5 _____

To God be the glory! I rejoice always! Thank you for my breath of life.

❑ I read my Bible.

❑ I am connected to God.

❑ I meditated for 15 min.

❑ I edited my words three times.

❑ I prayed.

☺

second the motion ☐

Date: _____

I write my thoughts, desires, and dreams down on paper. I journal.

I am grateful for:	What may I do differently to allow more happiness and peace in my life?
_____	_____
_____	_____
_____	_____
_____	**I have fun and celebrate this day by:**
_____	_____

I ask with intention for:

_____

_____

_____

_____

_____

_____ and more!

Why?

_____

_____

_____

_____

_____

My gains and miracles created:

_____

_____

_____

_____

1 _____
2 _____
3 _____
4 _____
5 _____

To God be the glory! I rejoice always! Thank you for my breath of life.

❏ I read my Bible.

❏ I am connected to God.

❏ I meditated for 15 min.

❏ I edited my words three times.

❏ I prayed.

☺

second the motion ☐

Date: _____

My love is like a beautiful rainbow that covers the whole sky.

I am grateful for:
_____
_____
_____
_____
_____

What may I do differently to allow more happiness and peace in my life?
_____
_____
_____

I have fun and celebrate this day by:
_____

I ask with intention for:
_____
_____
_____
_____
_____
_____ and more!

Why?
_____
_____
_____
_____
_____

My gains and miracles created:
_____
_____
_____
_____
_____

1 _____
2 _____
3 _____
4 _____
5 _____

To God be the glory! I rejoice always! Thank you for my breath of life.

- ❑ I read my Bible.
- ❑ I am connected to God.
- ❑ I meditated for 15 min.
- ❑ I edited my words three times.
- ❑ I prayed.

☺

second the motion

Date: _____

I receive joy.

I am grateful for:	What may I do differently to allow more happiness and peace in my life?
_____	_____
_____	_____
_____	_____
_____	**I have fun and celebrate this day by:**
_____	_____

I ask with intention for:	Why?
_____	_____
_____	_____
_____	_____
_____	_____
_____	_____
_____ and more!	_____

My gains and miracles created:	
_____	1 _____
_____	2 _____
_____	3 _____
_____	4 _____
_____	5 _____

To God be the glory! I rejoice always! Thank you for my breath of life.

❑ I read my Bible.

❑ I am connected to God.

❑ I meditated for 15 min.

❌ I edited my words three times.

❑ I prayed.

☺

second the motion ☐

Date: _____

God owns everything and he loves to share.
I ask continually and receive abundantly.

I am grateful for:
_____
_____
_____
_____
_____
_____

What may I do differently to allow more happiness and peace in my life?
_____
_____
_____

I have fun and celebrate this day by:
_____

I ask with intention for:
_____
_____
_____
_____
_____
_____ and more!

Why?
_____
_____
_____
_____
_____
_____

My gains and miracles created:
_____
_____
_____
_____
_____

1 _____
2 _____
3 _____
4 _____
5 _____

To God be the glory! I rejoice always! Thank you for my breath of life.

❏ I read my Bible.

❏ I am connected to God.

❏ I meditated for 15 min.

❏ I edited my words three times.

❏ I prayed.

☺

second the motion

Date: _____

I am fulfilled with my life and I show it to the world.

I am grateful for:
_____
_____
_____
_____
_____

What may I do differently to allow more happiness and peace in my life?
_____
_____
_____

I have fun and celebrate this day by:
_____

I ask with intention for:
_____
_____
_____
_____
_____
_____ and more!

Why?
_____
_____
_____
_____
_____

My gains and miracles created:
_____
_____
_____
_____
_____

1 _____
2 _____
3 _____
4 _____
5 _____

To God be the glory! I rejoice always! Thank you for my breath of life.

❑ I read my Bible.

❑ I am connected to God.

❑ I meditated for 15 min.

❑ I edited my words three times.

❑ I prayed.

☺

second the motion

Date: _____

I feel connected to a power that is greater than my individual self.

I am grateful for:
_____
_____
_____
_____
_____
_____

What may I do differently to allow more happiness and peace in my life?
_____
_____
_____

I have fun and celebrate this day by:
_____

I ask with intention for:
_____
_____
_____
_____
_____
_____ and more!

Why?
_____
_____
_____
_____
_____

My gains and miracles created:
_____
_____
_____
_____

1 _____
2 _____
3 _____
4 _____
5 _____

To God be the glory! I rejoice always! Thank you for my breath of life.

❏ I read my Bible.

❏ I am connected to God.

❏ I meditated for 15 min.

❏ I edited my words three times.

❏ I prayed.

☺

second the motion

Date: _____

I look within and see the loving, beautiful being I am.
I listen to my inner being.

I am grateful for:
_____
_____
_____
_____
_____

What may I do differently to allow more happiness and peace in my life?
_____
_____
_____

I have fun and celebrate this day by:
_____

I ask with intention for:
_____
_____
_____
_____
_____
_____ and more!

Why?
_____
_____
_____
_____
_____

My gains and miracles created:
_____
_____
_____
_____

1 _____
2 _____
3 _____
4 _____
5 _____

To God be the glory! I rejoice always! Thank you for my breath of life.

❑ I read my Bible.

❑ I am connected to God.

❑ I meditated for 15 min.

❑ I edited my words three times.

❑ I prayed.

☺

second the motion ☐

Date: _____

I can do everything and anything with God.

I am grateful for: _____ _____ _____ _____ _____ _____	What may I do differently to allow more happiness and peace in my life? _____ _____ _____ I have fun and celebrate this day by: _____

I ask with intention for: _____ _____ _____ _____ _____ _____ and more!	Why? _____ _____ _____ _____ _____ _____

My gains and miracles created: _____ _____ _____ _____ _____	1 _____ 2 _____ 3 _____ 4 _____ 5 _____

To God be the glory! I rejoice always! Thank you for my breath of life.

❑ I read my Bible.

❑ I am connected to God.

❑ I meditated for 15 min.

❑ I edited my words three times.

❑ I prayed.

☺

second the motion ☐

Date: _____

I am worthy. I deserve. The love I have for myself grows every day.

I am grateful for:	What may I do differently to allow more happiness and peace in my life?
_____	_____
_____	_____
_____	_____
_____	**I have fun and celebrate this day by:**
_____	_____

I ask with intention for:	Why?
_____	_____
_____	_____
_____	_____
_____	_____
_____	_____
_____ and more!	_____

My gains and miracles created:	
_____	1 _____
_____	2 _____
_____	3 _____
_____	4 _____
	5 _____

To God be the glory! I rejoice always! Thank you for my breath of life.

- ❑ I read my Bible.
- ❑ I am connected to God.
- ❑ I meditated for 15 min.
- ❑ I edited my words three times.
- ❑ I prayed.

☺

second the motion ☐

Date: _____

My heart is always singing and dancing.

I am grateful for:	What may I do differently to allow more happiness and peace in my life?
_____	_____
_____	_____
_____	_____
_____	**I have fun and celebrate this day by:**
_____	_____

I ask with intention for:	Why?
_____	_____
_____	_____
_____	_____
_____	_____
_____	_____
_____ and more!	_____

My gains and miracles created:	
_____	1 _____
_____	2 _____
_____	3 _____
_____	4 _____
_____	5 _____

To God be the glory! I rejoice always! Thank you for my breath of life.

❏ I read my Bible.

❏ I am connected to God.

❏ I meditated for 15 min.

❏ I edited my words three times.

❏ I prayed.

☺

second the motion ⬜

Date: _____

I am the co-creator of my life and the attractor of the wealth within it.

I am grateful for:	What may I do differently to allow more happiness and peace in my life?
_____	_____
_____	_____
_____	_____
_____	**I have fun and celebrate this day by:**
_____	_____

I ask with intention for:	Why?
_____	_____
_____	_____
_____	_____
_____	_____
_____	_____
_____ and more!	_____

My gains and miracles created:	
_____	1 _____
_____	2 _____
_____	3 _____
_____	4 _____
_____	5 _____

To God be the glory! I rejoice always! Thank you for my breath of life.

❑ I read my Bible.

❑ I am connected to God.

❑ I meditated for 15 min.

❑ I edited my words three times.

❑ I prayed.

☺

second the motion

Date: _____

I am living a wonderful life.

I am grateful for:	What may I do differently to allow more happiness and peace in my life?
_____	_____
_____	_____
_____	_____
_____	**I have fun and celebrate this day by:**
_____	_____

I ask with intention for:	Why?
_____	_____
_____	_____
_____	_____
_____	_____
_____	_____
_____ and more!	_____

My gains and miracles created:	
_____	1 _____
_____	2 _____
_____	3 _____
_____	4 _____
_____	5 _____

To God be the glory! I rejoice always! Thank you for my breath of life.

❑ I read my Bible.

❑ I am connected to God.

❑ I meditated for 15 min.

❑ I edited my words three times.

❑ I prayed.

☺

second the motion ⬜

Date: _____

I take ownership of all the goodness in my life right now.

I am grateful for:	What may I do differently to allow more happiness and peace in my life?
_____	_____
_____	_____
_____	_____
_____	**I have fun and celebrate this day by:**
_____	_____

I ask with intention for:	Why?
_____	_____
_____	_____
_____	_____
_____	_____
_____	_____
_____ and more!	_____

My gains and miracles created:	
_____	1 _____
_____	2 _____
_____	3 _____
_____	4 _____
_____	5 _____

To God be the glory! I rejoice always! Thank you for my breath of life.

❑ I read my Bible.

❑ I am connected to God.

❑ I meditated for 15 min.

❑ I edited my words three times.

❑ I prayed.

☺

second the motion ☐

Date: _____

I show gratitude and thanksgiving every day.

I am grateful for:
_____
_____
_____
_____
_____

What may I do differently to allow more happiness and peace in my life?
_____
_____
_____

I have fun and celebrate this day by:
_____

I ask with intention for:
_____
_____
_____
_____
_____
_____ and more!

Why?
_____
_____
_____
_____
_____

My gains and miracles created:
_____
_____
_____
_____

1 _____
2 _____
3 _____
4 _____
5 _____

To God be the glory! I rejoice always! Thank you for my breath of life.

❏ I read my Bible.

❏ I am connected to God.

❏ I meditated for 15 min.

❏ I edited my words three times.

❏ I prayed.

☺

second the motion ☐

Date: _____

All is well all the time.

I am grateful for:	What may I do differently to allow more happiness and peace in my life?
_____	_____
_____	_____
_____	_____
_____	**I have fun and celebrate this day by:**
_____	_____

I ask with intention for:	Why?
_____	_____
_____	_____
_____	_____
_____	_____
_____	_____
_____ and more!	_____

My gains and miracles created:	
_____	1 _____
_____	2 _____
_____	3 _____
_____	4 _____
_____	5 _____

To God be the glory! I rejoice always! Thank you for my breath of life.

❑ I read my Bible.

❑ I am connected to God.

❑ I meditated for 15 min.

❑ I edited my words three times.

❑ I prayed.

☺

second the motion ☐

Date: _____

I choose to focus only on the positive things I am creating.

I am grateful for:
_____
_____
_____
_____
_____
_____

What may I do differently to allow more happiness and peace in my life?
_____
_____
_____

I have fun and celebrate this day by:
_____

I ask with intention for:
_____
_____
_____
_____
_____
_____ and more!

Why?
_____
_____
_____
_____
_____
_____

My gains and miracles created:
_____
_____
_____
_____
_____

1 _____
2 _____
3 _____
4 _____
5 _____

To God be the glory! I rejoice always! Thank you for my breath of life.

❏ I read my Bible.

❏ I am connected to God.

❏ I meditated for 15 min.

❏ I edited my words three times.

❏ I prayed.

☺

second the motion

Date: _____

Love flows through me and touches everyone in my life.

I am grateful for:	What may I do differently to allow more happiness and peace in my life?
_____	_____
_____	_____
_____	_____
_____	**I have fun and celebrate this day by:**
_____	_____

I ask with intention for:	Why?
_____	_____
_____	_____
_____	_____
_____	_____
_____	_____
_____ and more!	_____

My gains and miracles created:	
_____	1 _____
_____	2 _____
_____	3 _____
_____	4 _____
_____	5 _____

To God be the glory! I rejoice always! Thank you for my breath of life.

❑ I read my Bible.

❑ I am connected to God.

❑ I meditated for 15 min.

❑ I edited my words three times.

❑ I prayed.

☺

second the motion ▢

Date: _____

I am glad. I rejoice in all.

I am grateful for:	What may I do differently to allow more happiness and peace in my life?
_____	_____
_____	_____
_____	_____
_____	**I have fun and celebrate this day by:**
_____	_____

I ask with intention for:	Why?
_____	_____
_____	_____
_____	_____
_____	_____
_____	_____
_____ and more!	_____

My gains and miracles created:	
_____	1 _____
_____	2 _____
_____	3 _____
_____	4 _____
_____	5 _____

To God be the glory! I rejoice always! Thank you for my breath of life.

❏ I read my Bible.

❏ I am connected to God.

❏ I meditated for 15 min.

❏ I edited my words three times.

❏ I prayed.

☺

second the motion ▢

Date: _____

I am wealthy. I am rich. I am happy.

I am grateful for:	What may I do differently to allow more happiness and peace in my life?
_____	_____
_____	_____
_____	_____
_____	**I have fun and celebrate this day by:**
_____	_____

I ask with intention for:	Why?
_____	_____
_____	_____
_____	_____
_____	_____
_____	_____
_____ and more!	_____

My gains and miracles created:	
_____	1 _____
_____	2 _____
_____	3 _____
_____	4 _____
_____	5 _____

To God be the glory! I rejoice always! Thank you for my breath of life.

❑ I read my Bible.

❑ I am connected to God.

❑ I meditated for 15 min.

❑ I edited my words three times.

❑ I prayed.

☺

second the motion ☐

Date: _____

My mouth smiles and speaks blessings.
My mind is clear and I have a fantastic memory.

I am grateful for:	What may I do differently to allow more happiness and peace in my life?
_____	_____
_____	_____
_____	_____
_____	**I have fun and celebrate this day by:**
_____	_____

I ask with intention for:	Why?
_____	_____
_____	_____
_____	_____
_____	_____
_____	_____
_____ and more!	_____

My gains and miracles created:	
_____	1 _____
_____	2 _____
_____	3 _____
_____	4 _____
_____	5 _____

To God be the glory! I rejoice always! Thank you for my breath of life.

❏ I read my Bible.

❏ I am connected to God.

❏ I meditated for 15 min.

❏ I edited my words three times.

❏ I prayed.

☺

second the motion ☐

Date: _____

I have God's powerful spirit within me.

I am grateful for:

_____

_____

_____

_____

What may I do differently to allow more happiness and peace in my life?

_____

_____

_____

I have fun and celebrate this day by:

_____

I ask with intention for:

_____

_____

_____

_____

_____

_____ and more!

Why?

_____

_____

_____

_____

_____

My gains and miracles created:

_____

_____

_____

_____

_____

1 _____

2 _____

3 _____

4 _____

5 _____

To God be the glory! I rejoice always! Thank you for my breath of life.

❑ I read my Bible.

❑ I am connected to God.

❑ I meditated for 15 min.

❑ I edited my words three times.

❑ I prayed.

☺

second the motion ▢

Date: _____

I choose to view my world friendly.

I am grateful for:	What may I do differently to allow more happiness and peace in my life?
_____	_____
_____	_____
_____	_____
_____	
_____	**I have fun and celebrate this day by:**
	_____

I ask with intention for:	Why?
_____	_____
_____	_____
_____	_____
_____	_____
_____	_____
_____ and more!	_____

My gains and miracles created:	
_____	1 _____
_____	2 _____
_____	3 _____
_____	4 _____
	5 _____

To God be the glory! I rejoice always! Thank you for my breath of life.

❑ I read my Bible.

❑ I am connected to God.

❑ I meditated for 15 min.

❑ I edited my words three times.

❑ I prayed.

☺

second the motion ▢

Date: _____

Because I come from love, I am love.

I am grateful for: _____ _____ _____ _____ _____	What may I do differently to allow more happiness and peace in my life? _____ _____ _____
	I have fun and celebrate this day by: _____

I ask with intention for:	Why?
_____ _____ _____ _____ _____ _____ and more!	_____ _____ _____ _____ _____

My gains and miracles created:	
_____ _____ _____ _____	1 _____ 2 _____ 3 _____ 4 _____ 5 _____

To God be the glory! I rejoice always! Thank you for my breath of life.

- ❑ I read my Bible.
- ❑ I am connected to God.
- ❑ I meditated for 15 min.
- ❑ I edited my words three times.
- ❑ I prayed.

☺

second the motion ☐

Date: _____

I always prosper in everything I do.

I am grateful for:	What may I do differently to allow more happiness and peace in my life?
_____	_____
_____	_____
_____	_____
_____	I have fun and celebrate this day by:
_____	_____

I ask with intention for:	Why?
_____	_____
_____	_____
_____	_____
_____	_____
_____	_____
_____ and more!	_____

My gains and miracles created:	
_____	1 _____
_____	2 _____
_____	3 _____
_____	4 _____
_____	5 _____

To God be the glory! I rejoice always! Thank you for my breath of life.

❏ I read my Bible.

❏ I am connected to God.

❏ I meditated for 15 min.

❏ I edited my words three times.

❏ I prayed.

☺

second the motion ☐

Date: _____

I choose to experience a harmonious day.

I am grateful for:	What may I do differently to allow more happiness and peace in my life?
_____	_____
_____	_____
_____	_____
_____	**I have fun and celebrate this day by:**
_____	_____

I ask with intention for:	Why?
_____	_____
_____	_____
_____	_____
_____	_____
_____	_____
_____ and more!	_____

My gains and miracles created:	
_____	1 _____
_____	2 _____
_____	3 _____
_____	4 _____
_____	5 _____

To God be the glory! I rejoice always! Thank you for my breath of life.

❑ I read my Bible.

❑ I am connected to God.

❑ I meditated for 15 min.

❑ I edited my words three times.

❑ I prayed.

☺

second the motion ☐

Date: _____

I welcome pure love into my heart.

I am grateful for:	What may I do differently to allow more happiness and peace in my life?
_____	_____
_____	_____
_____	_____
_____	**I have fun and celebrate this day by:**
_____	_____

I ask with intention for:	Why?
_____	_____
_____	_____
_____	_____
_____	_____
_____	_____
_____ and more!	_____

My gains and miracles created:	
_____	1 _____
_____	2 _____
_____	3 _____
_____	4 _____
_____	5 _____

To God be the glory! I rejoice always! Thank you for my breath of life.

❑ I read my Bible.

❑ I am connected to God.

❑ I meditated for 15 min.

❑ I edited my words three times.

❑ I prayed.

☺

second the motion ☐

Date: _____

God is good all the time.

I am grateful for:	What may I do differently to allow more happiness and peace in my life?
_____	_____
_____	_____
_____	_____
_____	**I have fun and celebrate this day by:**
_____	_____

I ask with intention for:	Why?
_____	_____
_____	_____
_____	_____
_____	_____
_____	_____
_____ and more!	_____

My gains and miracles created:	
_____	1 _____
_____	2 _____
_____	3 _____
_____	4 _____
_____	5 _____

To God be the glory! I rejoice always! Thank you for my breath of life.

❑ I read my Bible.

❑ I am connected to God.

❑ I meditated for 15 min.

❑ I edited my words three times.

❑ I prayed.

☺

second the motion

Date: _____

I am God's beautiful creation.

I am grateful for:
_____
_____
_____
_____
_____

What may I do differently to allow more happiness and peace in my life?
_____
_____
_____

I have fun and celebrate this day by:
_____

I ask with intention for:
_____
_____
_____
_____
_____
_____ and more!

Why?
_____
_____
_____
_____
_____

My gains and miracles created:
_____
_____
_____
_____

1 _____
2 _____
3 _____
4 _____
5 _____

To God be the glory! I rejoice always! Thank you for my breath of life.

❑ I read my Bible.

❑ I am connected to God.

❑ I meditated for 15 min.

❑ I edited my words three times.

❑ I prayed.

☺

second the motion

Date: _____

I rejoice always, and again I say rejoice.

I am grateful for:	What may I do differently to allow more happiness and peace in my life?
_____	_____
_____	_____
_____	_____
_____	**I have fun and celebrate this day by:**
_____	_____

I ask with intention for:	Why?
_____	_____
_____	_____
_____	_____
_____	_____
_____	_____
_____ and more!	_____

My gains and miracles created:	
_____	1 _____
_____	2 _____
_____	3 _____
_____	4 _____
_____	5 _____

To God be the glory! I rejoice always! Thank you for my breath of life.

❏ I read my Bible.

❏ I am connected to God.

❏ I meditated for 15 min.

❏ I edited my words three times.

❏ I prayed.

☺

second the motion ☐

Date: _____

I am worthy of having it all.
I am open to receive all the wealth life offers me.

I am grateful for:
_____
_____
_____
_____
_____

What may I do differently to allow more happiness and peace in my life?
_____
_____
_____

I have fun and celebrate this day by:
_____

I ask with intention for:
_____
_____
_____
_____
_____
_____ and more!

Why?
_____
_____
_____
_____
_____
_____

My gains and miracles created:
_____
_____
_____
_____

1 _____
2 _____
3 _____
4 _____
5 _____

To God be the glory! I rejoice always! Thank you for my breath of life.

❏ I read my Bible.

❏ I am connected to God.

❏ I meditated for 15 min.

❏ I edited my words three times.

❏ I prayed.

☺

second the motion ▢

Date: _____

My clear thinking and happy thoughts turn into a joyful performance each day.

I am grateful for:
_____
_____
_____
_____
_____

What may I do differently to allow more happiness and peace in my life?
_____
_____
_____

I have fun and celebrate this day by:
_____

I ask with intention for:
_____
_____
_____
_____
_____
_____ and more!

Why?
_____
_____
_____
_____
_____

My gains and miracles created:
_____
_____
_____
_____

1 _____
2 _____
3 _____
4 _____
5 _____

To God be the glory! I rejoice always! Thank you for my breath of life.

❑ I read my Bible.

❑ I am connected to God.

❑ I meditated for 15 min.

❑ I edited my words three times.

❑ I prayed.

☺

second the motion ☐

Date: _____

I live my divine purpose.

I am grateful for:	What may I do differently to allow more happiness and peace in my life?
_____	_____
_____	_____
_____	_____
_____	I have fun and celebrate this day by:
_____	_____

I ask with intention for:	Why?
_____	_____
_____	_____
_____	_____
_____	_____
_____	_____
_____ and more!	_____

My gains and miracles created:	
_____	1 _____
_____	2 _____
_____	3 _____
_____	4 _____
	5 _____

To God be the glory! I rejoice always! Thank you for my breath of life.

❑ I read my Bible.

❑ I am connected to God.

❑ I meditated for 15 min.

❑ I edited my words three times.

❑ I prayed.

☺

second the motion

Date: _____

I remain in peaceful harmony.

I am grateful for:	What may I do differently to allow more happiness and peace in my life?
_____	_____
_____	_____
_____	_____
_____	**I have fun and celebrate this day by:**
_____	_____

I ask with intention for:	Why?
_____	_____
_____	_____
_____	_____
_____	_____
_____	_____
_____ and more!	_____

My gains and miracles created:	
_____	1 _____
_____	2 _____
_____	3 _____
_____	4 _____
_____	5 _____

To God be the glory! I rejoice always! Thank you for my breath of life.

❏ I read my Bible.

❏ I am connected to God.

❏ I meditated for 15 min.

❏ I edited my words three times.

❏ I prayed.

☺

second the motion [ ]

Date: _____

I am aware of the words I am using.

I am grateful for:
_____
_____
_____
_____
_____

What may I do differently to allow more happiness and peace in my life?
_____
_____
_____

I have fun and celebrate this day by:
_____

I ask with intention for:
_____
_____
_____
_____
_____
_____ and more!

Why?
_____
_____
_____
_____
_____

My gains and miracles created:
_____
_____
_____
_____
_____

1 _____
2 _____
3 _____
4 _____
5 _____

To God be the glory! I rejoice always! Thank you for my breath of life.

❏ I read my Bible.

❏ I am connected to God.

❏ I meditated for 15 min.

❏ I edited my words three times.

❏ I prayed.

☺

second the motion

Date: _____

I truly love nature. I see beauty everywhere.

I am grateful for:	What may I do differently to allow more happiness and peace in my life?
_____	_____
_____	_____
_____	_____
_____	I have fun and celebrate this day by:
_____	_____

I ask with intention for:	Why?
_____	_____
_____	_____
_____	_____
_____	_____
_____	_____
_____ and more!	_____

My gains and miracles created:	
_____	1 _____
_____	2 _____
_____	3 _____
_____	4 _____
_____	5 _____

To God be the glory! I rejoice always! Thank you for my breath of life.

❑ I read my Bible.

❑ I am connected to God.

❑ I meditated for 15 min.

❑ I edited my words three times.

❑ I prayed.

☺

second the motion

Date: _____

I am filled with love and gratitude.

I am grateful for:	What may I do differently to allow more happiness and peace in my life?
_____	_____
_____	_____
_____	_____
_____	**I have fun and celebrate this day by:**
_____	_____

I ask with intention for:

_____

_____

_____

_____

_____

_____ and more!

Why?

_____

_____

_____

_____

_____

_____

My gains and miracles created:

_____

_____

_____

_____

1 _____
2 _____
3 _____
4 _____
5 _____

To God be the glory! I rejoice always! Thank you for my breath of life.

❑ I read my Bible.

❑ I am connected to God.

❑ I meditated for 15 min.

❑ I edited my words three times.

❑ I prayed.

☺

second the motion ☐

Date: _____

To God be the glory.

I am grateful for:	What may I do differently to allow more happiness and peace in my life?
_____	_____
_____	_____
_____	_____
_____	I have fun and celebrate this day by:
_____	_____

I ask with intention for:	Why?
_____	_____
_____	_____
_____	_____
_____	_____
_____	_____
_____ and more!	_____

My gains and miracles created:	
_____	1 _____
_____	2 _____
_____	3 _____
_____	4 _____
_____	5 _____

To God be the glory! I rejoice always! Thank you for my breath of life.

❑ I read my Bible.

❑ I am connected to God.

❑ I meditated for 15 min.

❑ I edited my words three times.

❑ I prayed.

☺

second the motion

Date: _____

I welcome money and prosperity in my life in every moment.

I am grateful for:	What may I do differently to allow more happiness and peace in my life?
_____	_____
_____	_____
_____	_____
_____	I have fun and celebrate this day by:
_____	_____
_____	

I ask with intention for:

_____
_____
_____
_____
_____
_____ and more!

Why?

_____
_____
_____
_____
_____
_____

My gains and miracles created:

_____
_____
_____
_____
_____

1 _____
2 _____
3 _____
4 _____
5 _____

To God be the glory! I rejoice always! Thank you for my breath of life.

❑ I read my Bible.

❑ I am connected to God.

❑ I meditated for 15 min.

❑ I edited my words three times.

❑ I prayed.

☺

second the motion ☐

Date: _____

I understand that water is the source of life and I can imprint it with beautiful loving messages.

I am grateful for:
_____
_____
_____
_____
_____

What may I do differently to allow more happiness and peace in my life?
_____
_____
_____

I have fun and celebrate this day by:
_____

I ask with intention for:
_____
_____
_____
_____
_____
_____ and more!

Why?
_____
_____
_____
_____
_____
_____

My gains and miracles created:
_____
_____
_____
_____
_____

1 _____
2 _____
3 _____
4 _____
5 _____

To God be the glory! I rejoice always! Thank you for my breath of life.

❑ I read my Bible.

❑ I am connected to God.

❑ I meditated for 15 min.

❑ I edited my words three times.

❑ I prayed.

☺

second the motion

Date: _____

I grow as I align with God.

I am grateful for:	What may I do differently to allow more happiness and peace in my life?
	I have fun and celebrate this day by:

I ask with intention for:

_____ and more!

Why?

My gains and miracles created:

1 _____
2 _____
3 _____
4 _____
5 _____

To God be the glory! I rejoice always! Thank you for my breath of life.

❑ I read my Bible.

❑ I am connected to God.

❑ I meditated for 15 min.

❑ I edited my words three times.

❑ I prayed.

☺

second the motion

Date: _____

I align my head with my heart.

I am grateful for:	What may I do differently to allow more happiness and peace in my life?
_____	_____
_____	_____
_____	_____
_____	**I have fun and celebrate this day by:**
_____	_____

I ask with intention for:	Why?
_____	_____
_____	_____
_____	_____
_____	_____
_____	_____
_____	_____
_____ and more!	_____

My gains and miracles created:	
_____	1 _____
_____	2 _____
_____	3 _____
_____	4 _____
_____	5 _____

To God be the glory! I rejoice always! Thank you for my breath of life.

❑ I read my Bible.

❑ I am connected to God.

❑ I meditated for 15 min.

❑ I edited my words three times.

❑ I prayed.

☺

second the motion ☐

Date: _____

I listen to and speak of excellent things.

I am grateful for:	What may I do differently to allow more happiness and peace in my life?
_____	_____
_____	_____
_____	_____
_____	**I have fun and celebrate this day by:**
_____	_____

I ask with intention for:	Why?
_____	_____
_____	_____
_____	_____
_____	_____
_____ and more!	_____

My gains and miracles created:	
_____	1 _____
_____	2 _____
_____	3 _____
_____	4 _____
_____	5 _____

To God be the glory! I rejoice always! Thank you for my breath of life.

❑ I read my Bible.

❑ I am connected to God.

❑ I meditated for 15 min.

❑ I edited my words three times.

❑ I prayed.

☺

second the motion ☐

Date: _____

I see only the good in myself and others.

I am grateful for:	What may I do differently to allow more happiness and peace in my life?
_____	_____
_____	_____
_____	_____
_____	**I have fun and celebrate this day by:**
_____	_____

I ask with intention for:	Why?
_____	_____
_____	_____
_____	_____
_____	_____
_____	_____
_____ and more!	_____

My gains and miracles created:	
_____	1 _____
_____	2 _____
_____	3 _____
_____	4 _____
_____	5 _____

To God be the glory! I rejoice always! Thank you for my breath of life.

❑ I read my Bible.

❑ I am connected to God.

❑ I meditated for 15 min.

❑ I edited my words three times.

❑ I prayed.

second the motion

Date: _____

I give thanks for each new day.

I am grateful for:

_____
_____
_____
_____
_____
_____

What may I do differently to allow more happiness and peace in my life?

_____
_____
_____

I have fun and celebrate this day by:

_____

I ask with intention for:

_____
_____
_____
_____
_____
_____ and more!

Why?

_____
_____
_____
_____
_____
_____

My gains and miracles created:

_____
_____
_____
_____
_____

1 _____
2 _____
3 _____
4 _____
5 _____

To God be the glory! I rejoice always! Thank you for my breath of life.

❑ I read my Bible.

❑ I am connected to God.

❑ I meditated for 15 min.

❑ I edited my words three times.

❑ I prayed.

☺

second the motion

Date: _____

I have great plans for my life and I write them down.

I am grateful for:	What may I do differently to allow more happiness and peace in my life?
_____	_____
_____	_____
_____	_____
_____	**I have fun and celebrate this day by:**
_____	_____

I ask with intention for:	Why?
_____	_____
_____	_____
_____	_____
_____	_____
_____	_____
_____ and more!	_____

My gains and miracles created:	
_____	1 _____
_____	2 _____
_____	3 _____
_____	4 _____
_____	5 _____

To God be the glory! I rejoice always! Thank you for my breath of life.

❑ I read my Bible.

❑ I am connected to God.

❑ I meditated for 15 min.

❑ I edited my words three times.

❑ I prayed.

☺

second the motion

Date: _____

I am mentally and emotionally able to enjoy a loving, prosperous life.
I am deeply fulfilled by all that I am.

I am grateful for:

_____
_____
_____
_____
_____
_____

What may I do differently to allow more happiness and peace in my life?

_____
_____
_____

I have fun and celebrate this day by:

_____

I ask with intention for:

_____
_____
_____
_____
_____
_____ and more!

Why?

_____
_____
_____
_____
_____

My gains and miracles created:

_____
_____
_____
_____

1 _____
2 _____
3 _____
4 _____
5 _____

To God be the glory! I rejoice always! Thank you for my breath of life.

❏ I read my Bible.

❏ I am connected to God.

❏ I meditated for 15 min.

❏ I edited my words three times.

❏ I prayed.

☺

second the motion

Date: _____

I am perfect exactly as I am right now.

I am grateful for:	What may I do differently to allow more happiness and peace in my life?
_____	_____
_____	_____
_____	_____
_____	**I have fun and celebrate this day by:**
_____	_____

I ask with intention for:	Why?
_____	_____
_____	_____
_____	_____
_____	_____
_____	_____
_____ and more!	_____

My gains and miracles created:	
_____	1 _____
_____	2 _____
_____	3 _____
_____	4 _____
_____	5 _____

To God be the glory! I rejoice always! Thank you for my breath of life.

- ❑ I read my Bible.
- ❑ I am connected to God.
- ❑ I meditated for 15 min.
- ❑ I edited my words three times.
- ❑ I prayed.

☺

second the motion [ ]

Date: _____

I am conscious of the words I speak.

I am grateful for:	What may I do differently to allow more happiness and peace in my life?
_____	_____
_____	_____
_____	_____
_____	**I have fun and celebrate this day by:**
_____	_____

I ask with intention for:	Why?
_____	_____
_____	_____
_____	_____
_____	_____
_____	_____
_____ and more!	_____

My gains and miracles created:	
_____	1 _____
_____	2 _____
_____	3 _____
_____	4 _____
_____	5 _____

To God be the glory! I rejoice always! Thank you for my breath of life.

❑ I read my Bible.

❑ I am connected to God.

❑ I meditated for 15 min.

❑ I edited my words three times.

❑ I prayed.

☺

second the motion

Date: _____

All my decisions stem from faith.

I am grateful for:	What may I do differently to allow more happiness and peace in my life?
_____	_____
_____	_____
_____	_____
_____	**I have fun and celebrate this day by:**
_____	_____

I ask with intention for:	Why?
_____	_____
_____	_____
_____	_____
_____	_____
_____	_____
_____ and more!	_____

My gains and miracles created:	1 _____
_____	2 _____
_____	3 _____
_____	4 _____
_____	5 _____

To God be the glory! I rejoice always! Thank you for my breath of life.

❑ I read my Bible.

❑ I am connected to God.

❑ I meditated for 15 min.

❑ I edited my words three times.

❑ I prayed.

☺

second the motion

Date: _____

I choose to remember only the good things.

I am grateful for:
_____
_____
_____
_____
_____
_____

What may I do differently to allow more happiness and peace in my life?
_____
_____
_____

I have fun and celebrate this day by:
_____

I ask with intention for:
_____
_____
_____
_____
_____
_____ and more!

Why?
_____
_____
_____
_____
_____
_____

My gains and miracles created:
_____
_____
_____
_____

1 _____
2 _____
3 _____
4 _____
5 _____

To God be the glory! I rejoice always! Thank you for my breath of life.

❑ I read my Bible.

❑ I am connected to God.

❑ I meditated for 15 min.

❑ I edited my words three times.

❑ I prayed.

☺

second the motion ⬜

Date: _____

I share perfect love and in return I receive perfect love.

I am grateful for:	What may I do differently to allow more happiness and peace in my life?
_____	_____
_____	_____
_____	_____
_____	**I have fun and celebrate this day by:**
_____	_____

I ask with intention for:	Why?
_____	_____
_____	_____
_____	_____
_____	_____
_____	_____
_____ and more!	_____

My gains and miracles created:	
_____	1 _____
_____	2 _____
_____	3 _____
_____	4 _____
	5 _____

To God be the glory! I rejoice always! Thank you for my breath of life.

❑ I read my Bible.

❑ I am connected to God.

❑ I meditated for 15 min.

❑ I edited my words three times.

❑ I prayed.

☺

second the motion

Date: _____

I am created in God's image.

I am grateful for:	What may I do differently to allow more happiness and peace in my life?
_____	_____
_____	_____
_____	_____
_____	**I have fun and celebrate this day by:**
_____	_____

I ask with intention for:	Why?
_____	_____
_____	_____
_____	_____
_____	_____
_____	_____
_____ and more!	_____

My gains and miracles created:	
_____	1 _____
_____	2 _____
_____	3 _____
_____	4 _____
_____	5 _____

To God be the glory! I rejoice always! Thank you for my breath of life.

❏ I read my Bible.

❏ I am connected to God.

❏ I meditated for 15 min.

❏ I edited my words three times.

❏ I prayed.

☺

second the motion ☐

Date: _____

I receive financial abundance by being who I am.

I am grateful for:
_____
_____
_____
_____
_____

What may I do differently to allow more happiness and peace in my life?
_____
_____
_____

I have fun and celebrate this day by:
_____

I ask with intention for:
_____
_____
_____
_____
_____
_____ and more!

Why?
_____
_____
_____
_____
_____

My gains and miracles created:
_____
_____
_____
_____

1 _____
2 _____
3 _____
4 _____
5 _____

To God be the glory! I rejoice always! Thank you for my breath of life.

❑ I read my Bible.

❑ I am connected to God.

❑ I meditated for 15 min.

❑ I edited my words three times.

❑ I prayed.

☺

second the motion

Date: _____

I believe in myself. I always see myself at my best.

I am grateful for:
_____
_____
_____
_____
_____
_____

What may I do differently to allow more happiness and peace in my life?
_____
_____
_____

I have fun and celebrate this day by:
_____

I ask with intention for:
_____
_____
_____
_____
_____
_____ and more!

Why?
_____
_____
_____
_____
_____

My gains and miracles created:
_____
_____
_____
_____

1 _____
2 _____
3 _____
4 _____
5 _____

To God be the glory! I rejoice always! Thank you for my breath of life.

❏ I read my Bible.

❏ I am connected to God.

❏ I meditated for 15 min.

❏ I edited my words three times.

❏ I prayed.

☺

second the motion

Date: _____

I understand that I am in co-creation with God.

I am grateful for:	What may I do differently to allow more happiness and peace in my life?
_____	_____
_____	_____
_____	_____
_____	I have fun and celebrate this day by:
_____	_____

I ask with intention for:	Why?
_____	_____
_____	_____
_____	_____
_____	_____
_____	_____
_____ and more!	_____

My gains and miracles created:	
_____	1_____
_____	2_____
_____	3_____
_____	4_____
_____	5_____

To God be the glory! I rejoice always! Thank you for my breath of life.

❑ I read my Bible.

❑ I am connected to God.

❑ I meditated for 15 min.

❑ I edited my words three times.

❑ I prayed.

☺

second the motion

Date: _____

I choose to see the good in all.

I am grateful for: _____ _____ _____ _____ _____	What may I do differently to allow more happiness and peace in my life? _____ _____ _____
	I have fun and celebrate this day by: _____

I ask with intention for: _____ _____ _____ _____ _____ and more!	Why? _____ _____ _____ _____ _____

My gains and miracles created: _____ _____ _____ _____	1 _____ 2 _____ 3 _____ 4 _____ 5 _____

To God be the glory! I rejoice always! Thank you for my breath of life.

❑ I read my Bible.

❑ I am connected to God.

❑ I meditated for 15 min.

❑ I edited my words three times.

❑ I prayed.

☺

second the motion ▢

Date: _____

I am alive, aware, joyous, and enthusiastic about life.

I am grateful for:	What may I do differently to allow more happiness and peace in my life?
_____	_____
_____	_____
_____	_____
_____	**I have fun and celebrate this day by:**
_____	_____

I ask with intention for:	Why?
_____	_____
_____	_____
_____	_____
_____	_____
_____	_____
_____ and more!	_____

My gains and miracles created:	
_____	1 _____
_____	2 _____
_____	3 _____
_____	4 _____
_____	5 _____

To God be the glory! I rejoice always! Thank you for my breath of life.

❑ I read my Bible.

❑ I am connected to God.

❑ I meditated for 15 min.

❑ I edited my words three times.

❑ I prayed.

☺

second the motion ☐

Date: _____

I only think positive thoughts about money, prosperity, and abundance.

I am grateful for:
_____
_____
_____
_____
_____

What may I do differently to allow more happiness and peace in my life?
_____
_____
_____

I have fun and celebrate this day by:
_____

I ask with intention for:
_____
_____
_____
_____
_____
_____ and more!

Why?
_____
_____
_____
_____
_____

My gains and miracles created:
_____
_____
_____
_____

1 _____
2 _____
3 _____
4 _____
5 _____

To God be the glory! I rejoice always! Thank you for my breath of life.

❏ I read my Bible.
❏ I am connected to God.
❏ I meditated for 15 min.
❏ I edited my words three times.
❏ I prayed.

☺

second the motion

Date: _____

My active body is transformed with my conscious mind.

I am grateful for:	What may I do differently to allow more happiness and peace in my life?
_____	_____
_____	_____
_____	_____
_____	**I have fun and celebrate this day by:**
_____	_____

I ask with intention for:	Why?
_____	_____
_____	_____
_____	_____
_____	_____
_____	_____
_____ and more!	_____

My gains and miracles created:	
_____	1 _____
_____	2 _____
_____	3 _____
_____	4 _____
_____	5 _____

To God be the glory! I rejoice always! Thank you for my breath of life.

❑ I read my Bible.

❑ I am connected to God.

❑ I meditated for 15 min.

❑ I edited my words three times.

❑ I prayed.

☺

second the motion [   ]

Date: _____

I am grateful and ready to live my day.

I am grateful for:	What may I do differently to allow more happiness and peace in my life?
_____	_____
_____	_____
_____	_____
_____	**I have fun and celebrate this day by:**
_____	_____

I ask with intention for:	Why?
_____	_____
_____	_____
_____	_____
_____	_____
_____	_____
_____ and more!	_____

My gains and miracles created:	
_____	1 _____
_____	2 _____
_____	3 _____
_____	4 _____
_____	5 _____

To God be the glory! I rejoice always! Thank you for my breath of life.

❏ I read my Bible.

❏ I am connected to God.

❏ I meditated for 15 min.

❏ I edited my words three times.

❏ I prayed.

☺

second the motion ☐

Date: _____

I am alive to experience God's greatness.

I am grateful for:	What may I do differently to allow more happiness and peace in my life?
_____	_____
_____	_____
_____	_____
_____	I have fun and celebrate this day by:
_____	_____

I ask with intention for:	Why?
_____	_____
_____	_____
_____	_____
_____	_____
_____	_____
_____ and more!	_____

My gains and miracles created:	
_____	1 _____
_____	2 _____
_____	3 _____
_____	4 _____
_____	5 _____

To God be the glory! I rejoice always! Thank you for my breath of life.

❑ I read my Bible.

❑ I am connected to God.

❑ I meditated for 15 min.

❑ I edited my words three times.

❑ I prayed.

second the motion

Date: _____

I am clear about what I intend for each day.
I write down what I welcome in each day.

I am grateful for:

_____

_____

_____

_____

_____

What may I do differently to allow more happiness and peace in my life?

_____

_____

_____

I have fun and celebrate this day by:

_____

I ask with intention for:

_____

_____

_____

_____

_____

_____ and more!

Why?

_____

_____

_____

_____

My gains and miracles created:

_____

_____

_____

_____

1 _____

2 _____

3 _____

4 _____

5 _____

To God be the glory! I rejoice always! Thank you for my breath of life.

❑ I read my Bible.

❑ I am connected to God.

❑ I meditated for 15 min.

❑ I edited my words three times.

❑ I prayed.

☺

second the motion [ ]

Date: _____

I love God and God loves me.

I am grateful for:	What may I do differently to allow more happiness and peace in my life?
_____	_____
_____	_____
_____	_____
_____	**I have fun and celebrate this day by:**
_____	_____

I ask with intention for:	Why?
_____	_____
_____	_____
_____	_____
_____	_____
_____	_____
_____	_____
_____ and more!	_____

My gains and miracles created:	
_____	1 _____
_____	2 _____
_____	3 _____
_____	4 _____
_____	5 _____

To God be the glory! I rejoice always! Thank you for my breath of life.

❑ I read my Bible.

❑ I am connected to God.

❑ I meditated for 15 min.

❑ I edited my words three times.

❑ I prayed.

☺

second the motion [ ]

Date: _____

I rejoice in You Jesus.

I am grateful for: _____ _____ _____ _____ _____ _____	What may I do differently to allow more happiness and peace in my life? _____ _____ _____
	I have fun and celebrate this day by: _____

I ask with intention for:	Why?
_____ _____ _____ _____ _____ _____ and more!	_____ _____ _____ _____ _____ _____

My gains and miracles created:	
_____ _____ _____ _____ _____	1 _____ 2 _____ 3 _____ 4 _____ 5 _____

To God be the glory! I rejoice always! Thank you for my breath of life.

❑ I read my Bible.

❑ I am connected to God.

❑ I meditated for 15 min.

❑ I edited my words three times.

❑ I prayed.

☺

second the motion ⬜

I declare that _I have the perfect jacket to give to_
my sister for Christmas.
_____

My parameters:

1. _ladies size small_
2. _waterproof_
3. _hood_
4. _lining_
5. _hip length_
6. _pockets_
7. _purple_
8. _on sale_

Why?

- _I am worthy and deserving._
- _I wish for my sister to receive the Christmas gift she desires._
- _She can use the rain jacket this week at Disney._
- _I love giving people gifts they desire._
- _I am a cheerful giver and receiver._

Thank you God, Jesus, and Holy Spirit!

I am so grateful that my sister has the perfect
Christmas gift.

I declare that _____

_____

_____

My parameters:

1. _____
2. _____
3. _____
4. _____
5. _____
6. _____
7. _____
8. _____

Why?

- _____
- _____
- _____
- _____
- _____

Thank you God, Jesus, and Holy Spirit!

_____

_____

I declare that _____

_____

_____

My parameters:

1. _____

2. _____

3. _____

4. _____

5. _____

6. _____

7. _____

8. _____

Why?

- _____

- _____

- _____

- _____

- _____

Thank you God, Jesus, and Holy Spirit!

_____

_____

I declare that _____

_____

_____

My parameters:

1. _____
2. _____
3. _____
4. _____
5. _____
6. _____
7. _____
8. _____

Why?

- _____
- _____
- _____
- _____
- _____

Thank you God, Jesus, and Holy Spirit!

_____

_____

I declare that _____

_____

_____

My parameters:

1. _____
2. _____
3. _____
4. _____
5. _____
6. _____
7. _____
8. _____

Why?

- _____
- _____
- _____
- _____
- _____

Thank you God, Jesus, and Holy Spirit!

_____

_____

I declare that _____

_____

_____

My parameters:

1. _____
2. _____
3. _____
4. _____
5. _____
6. _____
7. _____
8. _____

Why?

- _____
- _____
- _____
- _____
- _____

Thank you God, Jesus, and Holy Spirit!

_____

_____

I declare that _____

_____

_____

My parameters:

1. _____
2. _____
3. _____
4. _____
5. _____
6. _____
7. _____
8. _____

Why?

- _____
- _____
- _____
- _____
- _____

Thank you God, Jesus, and Holy Spirit!

_____

_____

I declare that _____

_____

_____

My parameters:

1. _____
2. _____
3. _____
4. _____
5. _____
6. _____
7. _____
8. _____

Why?

- _____
- _____
- _____
- _____
- _____

Thank you God, Jesus, and Holy Spirit!

_____

_____

I declare that _____

_____

_____

My parameters:

1. _____

2. _____

3. _____

4. _____

5. _____

6. _____

7. _____

8. _____

Why?

- _____

- _____

- _____

- _____

- _____

Thank you God, Jesus, and Holy Spirit!

_____

_____

I declare that _____

_____

_____

My parameters:

1. _____

2. _____

3. _____

4. _____

5. _____

6. _____

7. _____

8. _____

Why?

- _____

- _____

- _____

- _____

- _____

Thank you God, Jesus, and Holy Spirit!

_____

_____

I declare that _____

_____

_____

My parameters:

1. _____
2. _____
3. _____
4. _____
5. _____
6. _____
7. _____
8. _____

Why?

- _____
- _____
- _____
- _____
- _____

Thank you God, Jesus, and Holy Spirit!

_____

_____

I declare that _____

_____

_____

My parameters:

1. _____

2. _____

3. _____

4. _____

5. _____

6. _____

7. _____

8. _____

Why?

- _____

- _____

- _____

- _____

- _____

Thank you God, Jesus, and Holy Spirit!

_____

_____

I declare that _____

_____

_____

My parameters:

1. _____
2. _____
3. _____
4. _____
5. _____
6. _____
7. _____
8. _____

Why?

• _____

• _____

• _____

• _____

• _____

Thank you God, Jesus, and Holy Spirit!

_____

_____

I declare that _____

_____

_____

My parameters:

1. _____
2. _____
3. _____
4. _____
5. _____
6. _____
7. _____
8. _____

Why?

- _____
- _____
- _____
- _____
- _____

Thank you God, Jesus, and Holy Spirit!

_____

_____

I declare that _____

_____

_____

My parameters:

1. _____
2. _____
3. _____
4. _____
5. _____
6. _____
7. _____
8. _____

Why?

- _____
- _____
- _____
- _____
- _____

Thank you God, Jesus, and Holy Spirit!

_____

_____

I declare that _____

_____

_____

My parameters:

1. _____
2. _____
3. _____
4. _____
5. _____
6. _____
7. _____
8. _____

Why?

• _____

• _____

• _____

• _____

• _____

Thank you God, Jesus, and Holy Spirit!

_____

_____

I declare that _____

_____

_____

My parameters:

1. _____
2. _____
3. _____
4. _____
5. _____
6. _____
7. _____
8. _____

Why?

- _____
- _____
- _____
- _____
- _____

Thank you God, Jesus, and Holy Spirit!

_____

_____

I declare that _____

_____

_____

My parameters:

1. _____

2. _____

3. _____

4. _____

5. _____

6. _____

7. _____

8. _____

Why?

- _____

- _____

- _____

- _____

- _____

Thank you God, Jesus, and Holy Spirit!

_____

_____

I declare that _____

_____

_____

My parameters:

1. _____
2. _____
3. _____
4. _____
5. _____
6. _____
7. _____
8. _____

Why?

• _____

• _____

• _____

• _____

• _____

Thank you God, Jesus, and Holy Spirit!

_____

_____

I declare that _____

_____

_____

My parameters:

1. _____

2. _____

3. _____

4. _____

5. _____

6. _____

7. _____

8. _____

Why?

• _____

• _____

• _____

• _____

• _____

Thank you God, Jesus, and Holy Spirit!

_____

_____

I declare that _____

_____

_____

My parameters:

1. _____
2. _____
3. _____
4. _____
5. _____
6. _____
7. _____
8. _____

Why?

- _____
- _____
- _____
- _____
- _____

Thank you God, Jesus, and Holy Spirit!

_____

_____

I declare that _____

_____

_____

My parameters:

1. _____
2. _____
3. _____
4. _____
5. _____
6. _____
7. _____
8. _____

Why?

• _____

• _____

• _____

• _____

• _____

Thank you God, Jesus, and Holy Spirit!

_____

_____

I declare that _____

_____

_____

My parameters:

1. _____
2. _____
3. _____
4. _____
5. _____
6. _____
7. _____
8. _____

Why?

• _____

• _____

• _____

• _____

• _____

Thank you God, Jesus, and Holy Spirit!

_____

_____

I declare that _____

_____

_____

My parameters:

1. _____
2. _____
3. _____
4. _____
5. _____
6. _____
7. _____
8. _____

Why?

- _____

- _____

- _____

- _____

- _____

Thank you God, Jesus, and Holy Spirit!

_____

_____

I declare that _____

_____

_____

My parameters:

1. _____
2. _____
3. _____
4. _____
5. _____
6. _____
7. _____
8. _____

Why?

- _____
- _____
- _____
- _____
- _____

Thank you God, Jesus, and Holy Spirit!

_____

_____

I declare that _____

_____

_____

My parameters:

1. _____
2. _____
3. _____
4. _____
5. _____
6. _____
7. _____
8. _____

Why?

- _____
- _____
- _____
- _____
- _____

Thank you God, Jesus, and Holy Spirit!

_____

_____

I declare that _____

_____

_____

My parameters:

1. _____
2. _____
3. _____
4. _____
5. _____
6. _____
7. _____
8. _____

Why?

- _____
- _____
- _____
- _____
- _____

Thank you God, Jesus, and Holy Spirit!

_____

_____

I declare that _____

_____

_____

My parameters:

1. _____
2. _____
3. _____
4. _____
5. _____
6. _____
7. _____
8. _____

Why?

- _____
- _____
- _____
- _____
- _____

Thank you God, Jesus, and Holy Spirit!

_____

_____

I declare that _____

_____

_____

My parameters:

1. _____
2. _____
3. _____
4. _____
5. _____
6. _____
7. _____
8. _____

Why?

- _____

- _____

- _____

- _____

- _____

Thank you God, Jesus, and Holy Spirit!

_____

_____

I declare that _____

_____

_____

My parameters:

1. _____
2. _____
3. _____
4. _____
5. _____
6. _____
7. _____
8. _____

Why?

- _____
- _____
- _____
- _____
- _____

Thank you God, Jesus, and Holy Spirit!

_____

_____

I declare that _____

_____

_____

My parameters:

1. _____
2. _____
3. _____
4. _____
5. _____
6. _____
7. _____
8. _____

Why?

- _____
- _____
- _____
- _____
- _____

Thank you God, Jesus, and Holy Spirit!

_____

_____

Notes

Notes

Notes

Notes

Notes

Notes

Notes

Notes

Notes

Notes

Receive Joy seconds the motion for everything good and more that you desire to consciously create with this *Daily Asking Journal.*

This *Daily Asking Journal* helps to develop a daily practice of the Nine Step Method presented in the book *Ask And You Shall Receive* by Receive Joy (ISBN 9780998848488). The book and journal are available directly from Receive Joy ($15 and $10, respectively plus shipping) or order on amazon.

We also recorded an uplifting 20-minute *Ask And You Shall Receive Mediation CD* in all positive words. The CD is available directly from Receive Joy. ($5 plus shipping)

To learn more visit **www.receivejoy.com**

Subscribe to our newsletter to continue your receiving of positive awareness. Please share your email address with us. Send us a message over the contact page of the website or directly to **ask@receivejoy.com**

Call or text to US cell phone number **(239) 450-1240**.

Like and follow Receive Joy on Facebook: **www.facebook.com/ReceiveJoy**

Follow Receive Joy on Instagram: **www.instagram.com/receivejoy**

We are happy to hear from you and receive your positive feedback, inspiration, and miracle stories!

Made in the USA
Columbia, SC
16 November 2017